CW00495927

JANEY GODLEY (www.janeygodley.com) has had over 50 million online hits for her iconic voiceover videos. A former Scotswoman of the Year nominee and a *Scotsman* columnist, she has been a guest on the BBC radio series *Just a Minute* and *Loose Ends* and has been popping up on the television panel show *Have I Got News For You*, and recently on BBC Radio 4 with her own half-hour comedy special.

Janey's short film *The Last Mermaid*, directed by Fi Kelley, has won various awards at film festivals across the globe. She has performed in the multi-award winning movie *Wild Rose* and in *Traces* (Alibi channel), as well as writing and acting for the National Theatre of Scotland. Her first novel *Nothing Left Unsaid* was published recently.

Over this past year, as Janey underwent treatment for ovarian cancer, Wee Honey has been by her side every step of the way. She is now on the road to recovery – partly due to the fact that Wee Honey took every opportunity to cuddle and love her when she was feeling low.

Honey still rules the house.

## By the same author

*Handstands in the Dark: A True Story of Growing Up and Survival* (Ebury Press, 2006)
*Frank get the door, ma feet are killin me!* (Luath Press, 2020)
*Nothing Left Unsaid* (Hodder & Stoughton, 2022)
*Honey Found a Home – the lucky sausage* (Luath Press, 2022)

## Praise for Janey Godley

*She's a bold, take-no-prisoners type of comic, totally honest and hilarious with it.*—EDINBURGH EVENING NEWS

*Janey Godley is the most outspoken female stand-up in Britain.*
—DAILY TELEGRAPH

*Clever, passionate and lyrical*—DAILY MIRROR

*Many thanks for helping keep the nation's spirits up. I'm a big fan, and also love sausage dogs.*—SHELAGH FRASER

*I'm an over-friendly cleaner who talks too much.*
—JANEY GODLEY

# Honey and Janey
## you've been telt!

JANEY GODLEY

**Luath** Press Limited

EDINBURGH

www.luath.co.uk

First published 2022

ISBN: 978-1-910022-69-6

The author's right to be identified as author of this book
under the Copyright, Designs and Patents Act 1988
has been asserted.

Printed and bound by
Gutenberg Press Ltd., Malta

Typeset and designed by
Main Point Books, Edinburgh

© Janey Godley 2022

# Introduction

## Janey Godley

IN 2017, MY daughter Ashley told me a lady was giving away her wee dog and was looking for a nice home for it and she asked could we take it in?

I wasn't sure if we could give a home to dog that has already been through a family. I thought, maybe we should get a wee puppy and start from there?

Then again, I didn't want a dog, as we have such busy lives and my husband repeatedly told me, 'I don't want a dog.' So we decided we didn't want a dog and made the family decision to one day own a cat and work towards that.

That March night of 2017, Ashley went to see the lady who owned the dog to explain her position and offer to help her find a home for the wee sausage on social media. 'Someone will want it. Mum will post a picture of her,' Ashley added.

Ashley met this dog in the woman's house. The wee beastie ran and barked at her, then licked her hand.

So that night we got a dog. Of course, Ashley fell in love at first sight with the wee angry croissant that snarled at her then wagged her tail.

I came back from a comedy gig and there on the sofa was a wee tan-coloured sausage dog called Honey. She looked scared. She sat shivering on Ashley's knee and barked at me. Husband was very annoyed at this situation, as he didn't want a dog (remember?). But immediately the wee sausage crawled off Ashley's knee and climbed up husband's chest and mouth-kissed him, love was instant.

My husband lives with autism and for some reason this wee grumpy, stumpy-legged dog makes his world feel better. They are inseparable.

Honey has a scar and a lump on her belly which looks like the result of a difficult birth. We don't know much about how many puppies she had, or her past health issues, but within months of coming to live with us, she almost died of an auto-immune disease. She pulled through, a hernia was repaired and she was neutered and chipped. Get pet insurance is all I can tell you!

Honey has become the Queen of our house. She can walk two miles a day and then we push her in a pram, which she absolutely adores. She gets fed the best of chicken and lovely treats. There are ramps so she can go everywhere she wants. Her every need is our mission to accomplish.

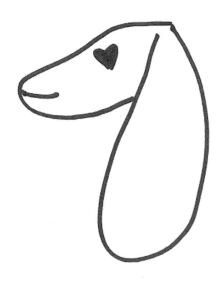

Honey has starred in many videos and on TV she has appeared with Ashley in her show *Up for It;* and of course with me in *Alone,* one of the National Theatre of Scotland *Scenes for Survival* short plays. She is a natural.

I don't know what would have happened if Ashley hadn't found Honey. We probably would never have gotten a dog. I am glad we did – our lives are so much richer for having wee Honey, so we wanted to share some of that with you. Enjoy the book!

*Janey*

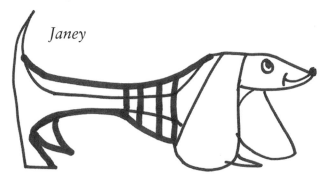

# Introduction

## Honey

ONE NIGHT I was in my house and a tall lady with a lot of hair came in, so I showed her who's boss and snarled. She picked me up and took me in a car and sat me on her knee. I thought I had been kidnapped – you hear so much about this on the news and now it was happening to me. The lady with lots of hair sang old-timey jazz tunes to me as the car drove off, and she blew raspberries into my cheeks, which is my favourite thing. (Not many people know that, but she must have known somehow.)

Anyway, she brought me to a new house and I wasn't sure who had stolen me and if my owners would find me, so I was a bit scared. I peed the carpet in protest. They never got angry.

I wasn't very well but I couldn't tell if these new people would know, so I sat quiet. Then a loud chubby lady arrived, she is really loud and takes up all the space in the room, so I barked at her and showed her all my sharp teeth. That'll make her shut up, I thought. It didn't.

There was a very quiet man I liked on sight. He didn't sing or talk loudly, so I gave him kisses. We became friends immediately and he took me away from the two women and put me on his bed and wrapped me in a blanket and we listened to a radio show in the dark. It was lovely. He must need to do this a lot with two such loud ladies in his house.

This is what I have worked out about my kidnappers. The tall one is called Ashley and she is very young and not responsible. I think she is still a child, as she is very clumsy and likes spaceships (I have been in her room). She is good at singing and can't tie her laces.

The chubby loud one is Janey, she is very easy to manipulate and I get her to give me her food when nobody is looking. She got me so fat the vet pointed a finger at her. She makes videos of me and I like that.

The man is called 'Him' and he weighs all my food and he built ramps so I could run up and down in his house. Apparently he doesn't want a dog, so now I am worried he will stop being my kidnapper and give me back to the people who used to own me. But I don't want to go back, I like it here.

Ashley told me, 'You are our dog now, we love you and you can stay here.' That made me happy.

'Him' bought me a pram and I can now see the

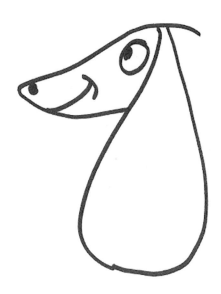

whole city tucked up safely in my chariot. He walks me for miles. Janey takes me to cafés and feeds me titbits. I am a lucky sausage.

I hate pigeons and seagulls so Janey waves them away. She shouts words that I never heard in my previous home. I think she might be bilingual.

Actually, I am scared of people. Once I nearly died and ended up in hospital beside a very sad cat called Sooty and we became pals. But now I live my life happily with the strange, loud, shouty family.

'Him' told me he would always be my pal and now I sleep in the crook of his arm and Janey feeds me chicken and Ashley sings into my cheeks.

I am lucky.

I hope you like this book and all my nice photos.

*Honey*

WEE
HONEY DRESSED
LIKE "WEE SADIE"

CUTE FACE

WHEN YOU ARE Scrubbing DOG SHIT off THE SHAG PILE CARPET and YOU see this

Yes I know I have

**SHAT**

on your **MAT**

JANEY you still love me

**don't you?**

THis wasn't
what she was
WATCHING, she
CliCKEd it over
from "Doggie STYLE"

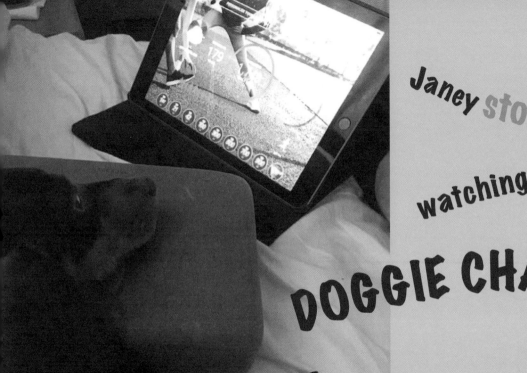

Janey stopped me watching my fave DOGGIE CHANNEL

HER WEE CUTE PAWS. AW FUCK THE FLASH IS ON.... BUT LOOK at HER WEE PAWS

FUCKSAKE
TURN THE FLASH OFF
. . . and will you
SHUT UP
about my paws!

NOTHING EVER
FITS ME
BUT
EVERYTHING FITS
HONEY

There's a shop that sells

DOG clothes

and guess

where I have to go

EVERY DAY

THIS IS THE
BEST PLACE
FOR A
PISS!

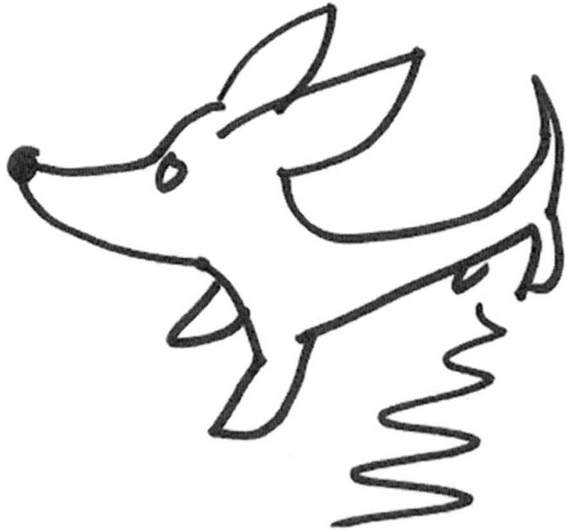

Sometimes **Janey** gets caught short *al fresco*

I HAD a Jumper like THIS IN THE '80s and it itCHED LikE FUck

When your auntie **knits it**
you have to **wear it**

Took me AGES
TO GET HONEY
TO KEEP THIS
FUCKing OUTFIT ON
SO SHE PEED!!

HAllOWEEN

Well it is a

PISS-POOR

skeleton outfit

WHO LOVES A DUG CLAW UP YOUR NOSTRIL?

ME.... ESPECIALLY IN MY SLEEP

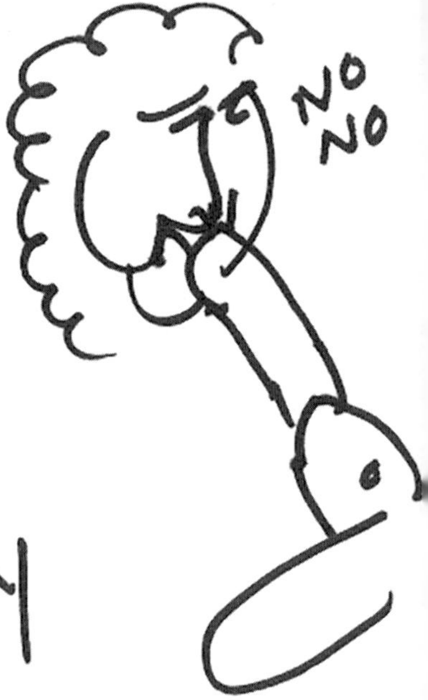

If JANEY doesn't wake up

to FEED ME

I PUNCH her

If a sausage
dog was
Bet Lynch
from CORRIE

Corrie???

This is me ready for

STRICTLY

COME SAUSAGE

NEVER
Fucking lift
a Dog up like
THIS!

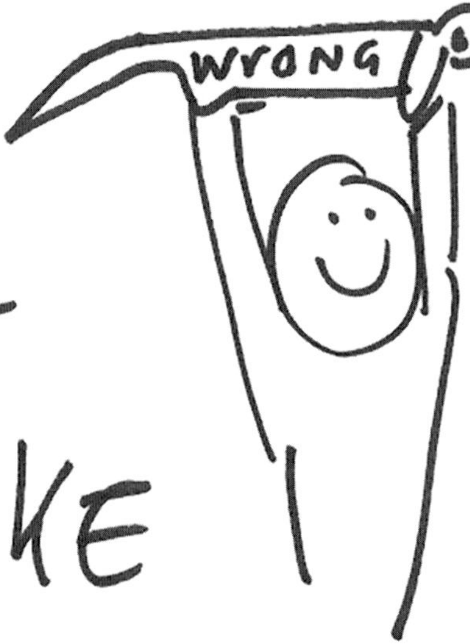

PUT ME DOWN
you CRAZY LADY

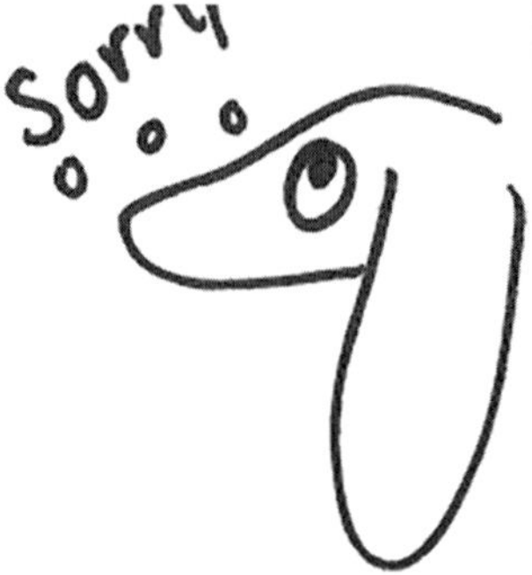


SHE PEED
All over the
sofa ....
But look at her
face

CUTE

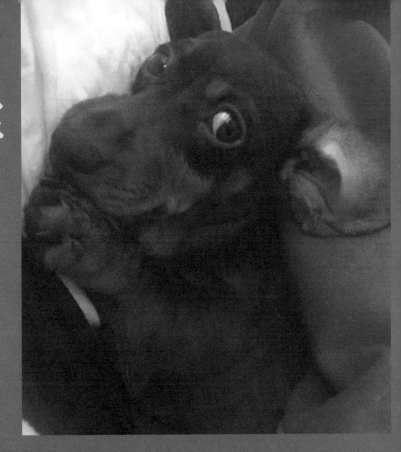

When I pull this
CUTE FACE

Janey forgets
and forgives

WHEN YOU
Find that
ONE
OUTFIT !

Long hair suits me

might get some extensions

I like to
DReSS HONEY
AS SENGA
going to THE
STEAMIE

HONEY
PISSED
IN MY SUITCASE
AND LAUGHED

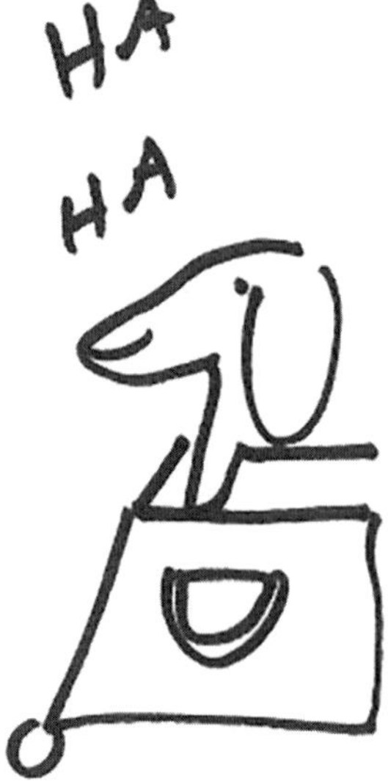

Ha ha! my TONGUE IS that long

WHEN YOUR
Dug looks
better in your
clothes
than you do!

ALWAYS

*wear a colour*

**that compliments**

your skin tone

How can she
be so?
SHiNY?
THE cash Ispent
on hair serum!

How **LUCKY** is Janey to have such a

# GLOSSY DOG

I ATE A CAKE
AND HONEY CRIED
THE WHOLE
Fucking TiME

Liar Liar
CHUNKY BUM
She scoffed THREE cakes
and I never got a
CRUMB

I knew I would
end up
with a dog
Jumper

Who but JANEY would have TWO ARAN JUMPERS THIS SMALL?

HONEY
HATED THE
PINEAPPLE...
It was too JAggY

Fucking
NAILED
oriGAMi

SHE loves TO
STARE WHEN
I EAT.

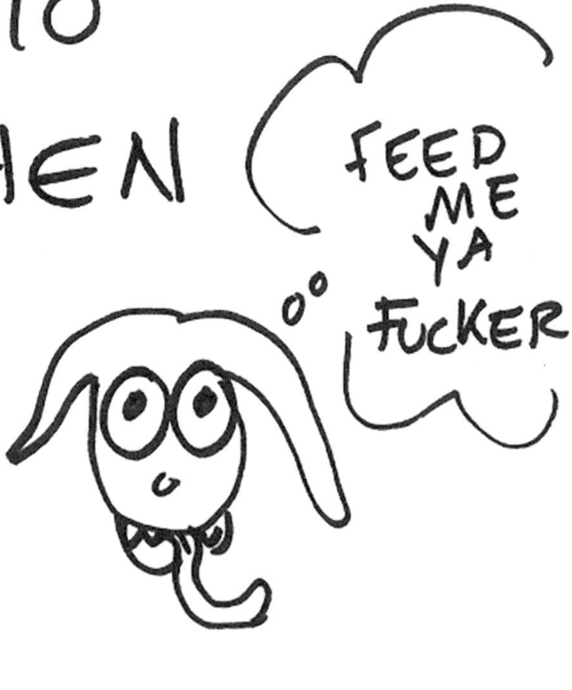

Watching Janey *eat* makes me HUNGRY so I'll STARE at the DOG BISCUIT TIN

WEE
FUCKER IS IN
MY FRIDGE!!

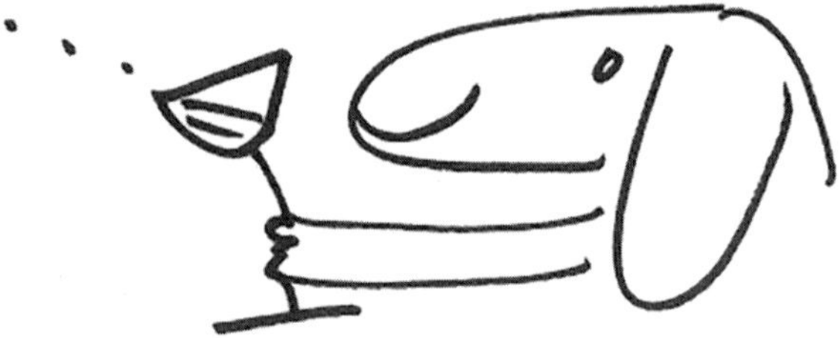

You can keep that **CHAMPAGNE** in the fridge door

I'm after the Honey Roast **ham!**

Honey is Available for Dinner Dates and Weddings

WEE
CREEPY
FUCKER
BARKING at
SHADOWS

I love to wind Janey up

by pretending to see a GHOST

HONEY HELPS
ME TO DIET
by guilting
Every Fucking
mouthful of Food

I LOVE CAKE

& you've exceeded

your calories

HAND IT OVER!

# Honey is as good at football as the Scotland Squad

#Rubbish

What are you on about Janey?

I'm training for the

SCOTLAND
SAUSAGE SQUAD

SHE looks like
A WEE woman
called Margaret
who MISSED HER
Turn at THE STeamie

That NOISE from these FUCKERS NEXT DOOR makes me want to PISS through their LETTERBOX

# HONEY LOVES SHARING THE PRAM

I get NOTHING from the deli but ROLY POLY gets a WHOLE cannoli

WHEN YOUR DUG WATCHES TOO MUCH TELLY

They say
'WINTER IS COMING'
but here in GLASGOW
it's ALWAYS FUCKING WINTER

Look out it's

## MADONNA!

I strike this pose

to annoy Janey

cos she SHE can't do it

WHEN YOU WALK IN and THINK "THis is not my business"

STAY STILL
Teddy

I'm trying to
CUDDLE YOU

ICE CREAM
For DUGS

WHEN THE FUCK
Did that happen?

ANY ice cream is
DOG ice cream

ME
CRUSHING
TWITTER
as HONEY
lEARNS NEW
SWEARS

Fuck!

You're barking Janey

I know more SWEARS than YOU

ANY FUCKING DAY

I got bored
and the
Amazon man
brought
headbonds

NO NO NO

They gave me the ANNE BOLEYN LOOK for SHITS & GIGGLES

Honey
loves
CHRISTMAS
I love THAT JUMPER
Got My money's WORTH

Merry Christmas from Honey

AS USUAL

I get SLAPPED ON

a shitty Photoshop

I USED TO
Fantasise ABOUT
GEORGE Clooney...
NOW THIS IS MY
life —

My name is SHADOW
HONEY SHADOW
licensed to kill
SMALL BEETLES

like SHE DOESN't GET ENOUGH ATTENTION

**BORED** OUT MY BOX

**WHY**

has Janey got to speak

to **every fucker**
she meets?

ME AND HONEY

JANEY

HONEY

Me and Janey
in one photo
for HALLOWEEN

I ONLY LEFT ASHLEY IN THE SHOP ONCE!

It's like that time Janey forgot Ashley

Now it's my turn

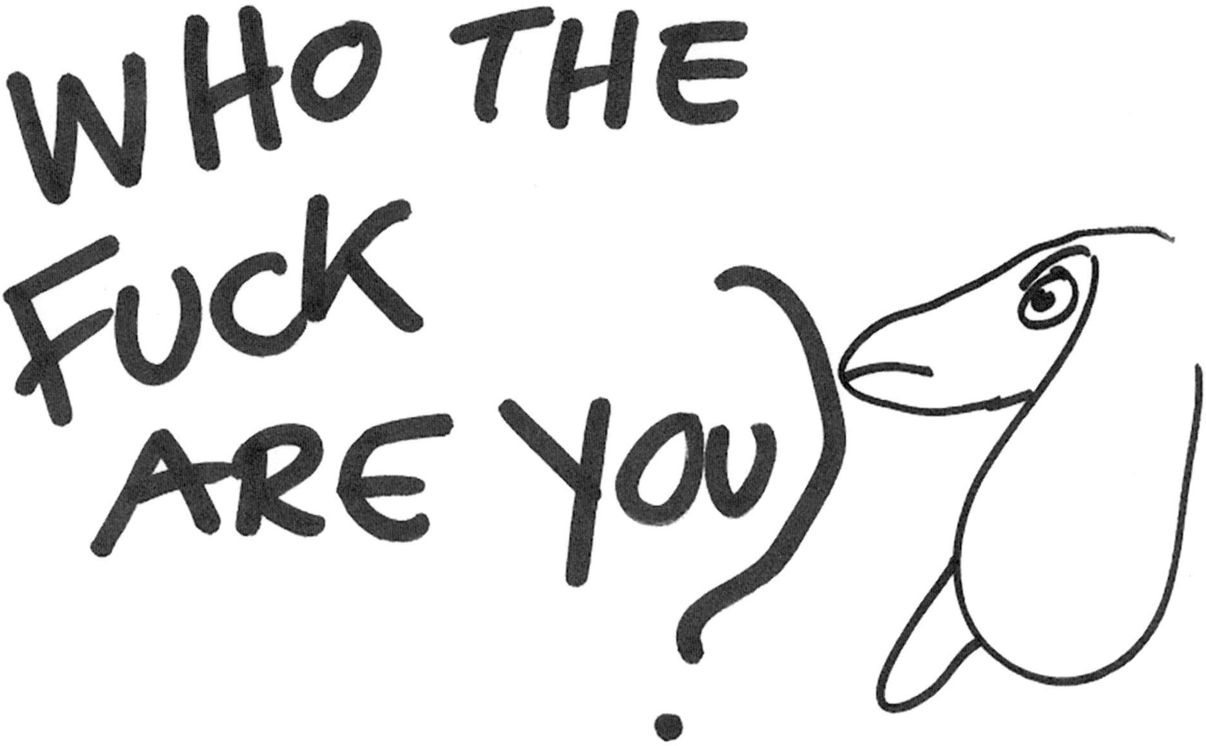
WHO THE FUCK ARE YOU?

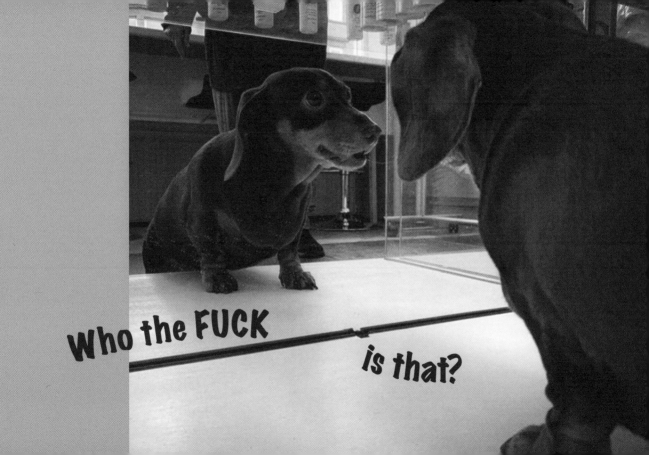

THE
VACCINE
TASTES of
BEEF?

Janey says she's not been MICROCHIPPED

but all the

best dogs are

What are you making?

It better be for me!

She WANTS To go with ME, EVERYTIME

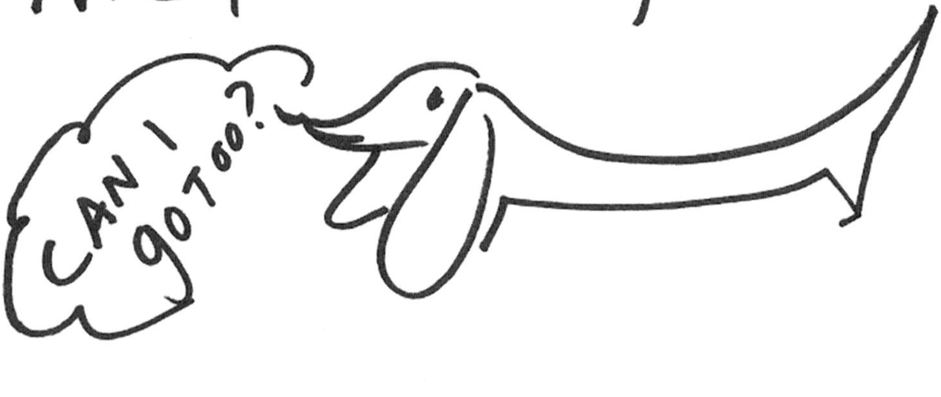

GOING OUT

without ME

Janey?

expect a SHIT!

IN YOUR GOOD SHOES

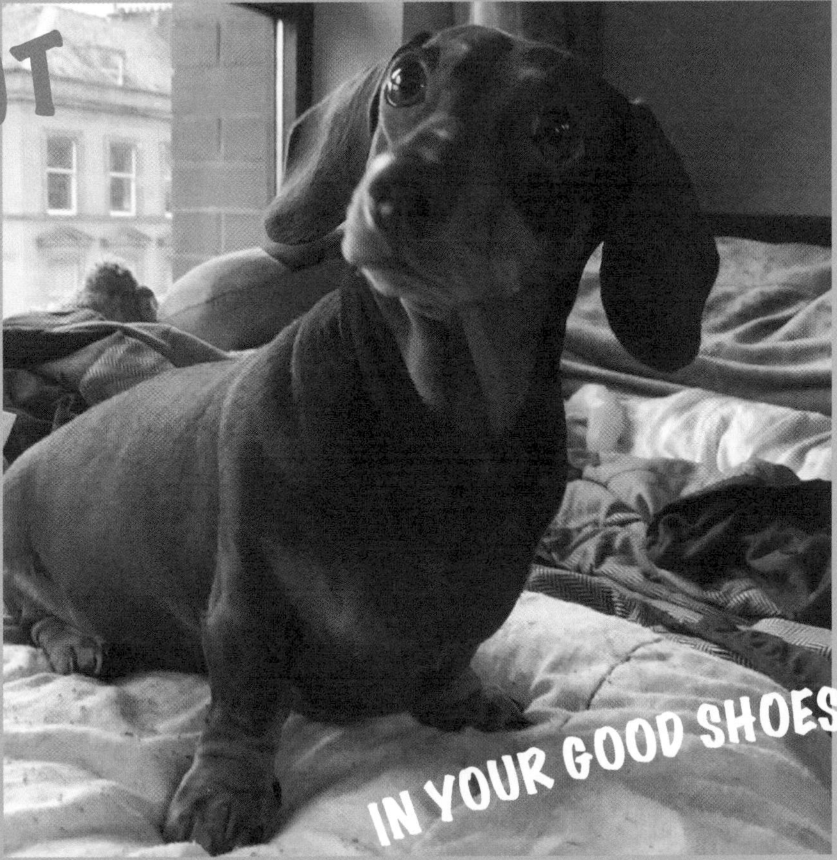

SHE ALMOST CHOKED ON THIS SLABBERY BONE

Janey

TOOK THIS OFF ME

First chance I get
I will choke HER

WHAT THE FUCK DO YOU WANT HONEY?

HELLO BOYS

Janey has promised me a **KILT**

She must think I'm a Scotty dog

SHE HAS WATCHED TOO MANY love FILMS

ROMANCE

Stay still
YOU BEADY-EYED FUCKER

and let me
CHIN YOU

MY NIPS ARE FREEZING

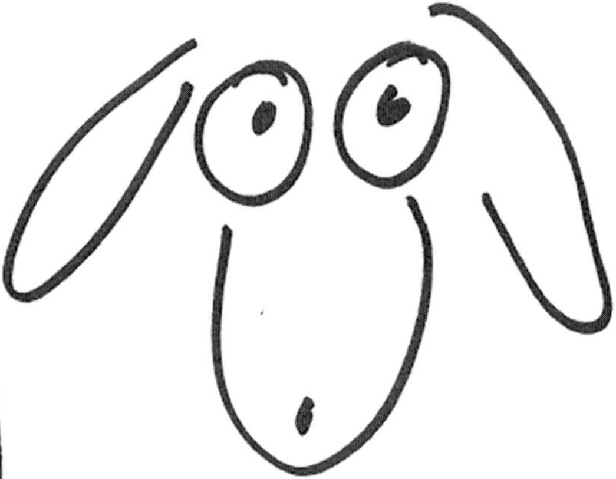

TOO

CANNAE
BE FUCKED
WITH CHRISTMAS
THIS IS AS GOOD
AS it gets

Cheapo Janey's

Christmas tree

makes me look giant

WHEN YOU
HAVE
NO
ACTUAL
PHOTOS
OF YOUR GRANNY

SERIOUSLY
I Look better
in hairbands
than Janey

Who doesn't love
A Dug Paw in
your EYE as
you Sleep?

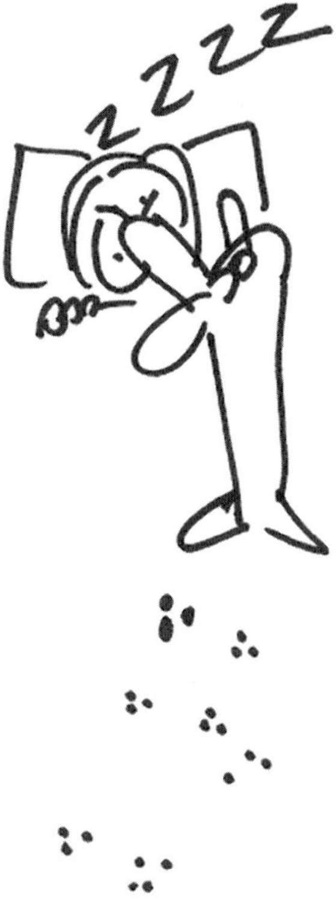

SHUT UP NOBODY wants your comedy

# Canine Charities

Edinburgh Dog and Cat Home
26 Seafield Road East
Edinburgh EH15 1EH
https://edch.org.uk
0131 699 5331
Scottish Charity No. SC 006914

Scottish Society for the Prevention of
Cruelty to Animals (Scottish SPCA)
Kingseat Road
Halbeath
Dunfermline
Fife KY11 8RY
https://www.scottishspca.org
03000 999 999
Scottish Charity No. SC 006467

Scottish SPCA Animal Rescue and Rehoming Centre
Drumoak
Mains of Drum
Banchory
Aberdeenshire AB31 5AJ
https://www.scottishspca.org/our-work/aberdeenshire
03000 999 999
Scottish Charity No. SC 006467

Edinburgh Samoyed Rescue
Earl Grey Street
Edinburgh EH3 9BN
https://www.edinburghsamoyedrescue.com
0131 531 6687
Scottish Charity No. SC 048163

Scottish SPCA Edinburgh & Lothians
Animal Rescue & Rehoming Centre
Lothian Animal Welfare Centre
Manfield Road
Balerno
Edinburgh EH14 7JU
https://www.scottishspca.org
03000 999 999
Scottish Charity No. SC 006467

Dog Aid Society of Scotland
60 Blackford Avenue
Edinburgh EH9 3ER
https://www.dogaidsociety.com
0131 668 3633
Scottish Charity No. SC 001918

Perthshire Abandoned Dogs Society (PADS)
Station House Road
Forteviot
Perth PH2 9BS
https://padsdogrescue.com
01764 684 491
Scottish Charity No. SC 011033

Greyhound Rescue Fife
Baltree Country Centre
Gairneybank
Kinross KY13 0LF
http://www.greyhoundrescuefife.com
01577 850 393
Scottish Charity No. SC 044047

Second Chance Kennels
Balbegie Avenue
Thornton
Fife KY1 3NS
https://www.secondchancekennels.org
01592 771 933
Scottish Charity No. SC 032202

Dogs Trust Glasgow
315 Hamilton Road
Uddingston
Glasgow G71 7SL
https://www.dogstrust.org.uk/our-centres/glasgow
0303 003 0000
Scottish Charity No. SC 037843

Dogs Trust West Calder
Bentyhead
West Calder
West Lothian EH55 8LE
https://www.dogstrust.org.uk/our-centres/west-calder
01506 873 459
Scottish Charity No. SC 037843

Canine Concern Scotland Trust (CCST)
81-85 Portland Street
Edinburgh EH6 4AY
https://www.canineconcernscotland.org.uk
0131 553 0034
Scottish Charity No. SC 014924

Dumfries & Galloway Canine Rescue Centre
Dovecotwells
by Glencaple
Dumfries DG1 4RH
https://www.caninerescue.co.uk
01387 770 210
Scottish Charity No. SC 031991

D.A.W.G.S.
'The Dawghouse'
The Old Bakehouse
Main Street
Alford AB33 8PX
http://dawgs.co.uk
01224 208 989
Scottish Charity No. SC 022666

Borders Pet Rescue
Earlston
Scottish Borders TD4 6DJ
https://www.borderspetrescue.org
01896 849 090
Scottish Charity No. SC 350506

Loving Homes Dog Rescue
Graemeshall Farmhouse
Holm
Orkney KW17 2RX
http://www.lovinghomesdogrescue.org.uk
01856 781 589
Scottish Charity No. SC 047453

Canine Campus Pet Rescue
2 Hamilton Road
Glasgow G73 3DG
https://www.canine-campus.org
07564 303 008
Scottish Charity No. SC 047945

# **Luath** Press Limited

*committed to publishing well written books worth reading*

LUATH PRESS takes its name from Robert Burns, whose little collie Luath (*Gael.*, swift or nimble) tripped up Jean Armour at a wedding and gave him the chance to speak to the woman who was to be his wife and the abiding love of his life. Burns called one of the 'Twa Dogs' Luath after Cuchullin's hunting dog in Ossian's *Fingal*. Luath Press was established in 1981 in the heart of Burns country, and is now based a few steps up the road from Burns' first lodgings on Edinburgh's Royal Mile. Luath offers you distinctive writing with a hint of unexpected pleasures.

Most bookshops in the UK, the US, Canada, Australia, New Zealand and parts of Europe, either carry our books in stock or can order them for you. To order direct from us, please send a £sterling cheque, postal order, international money order or your credit card details (number, address of cardholder and expiry date) to us at the address below. Please add post and packing as follows: UK – £1.00 per delivery address; overseas surface mail – £2.50 per delivery address; overseas airmail – £3.50 for the first book to each delivery address, plus £1.00 for each additional book by airmail to the same address. If your order is a gift, we will happily enclose your card or message at no extra charge.

**Luath** Press Limited
543/2 Castlehill
The Royal Mile
Edinburgh EH1 2ND
Scotland
Telephone: 0131 225 4326 (24 hours)
Fax: 0131 225 4324
email: sales@luath.co.uk
Website: www.luath.co.uk